Bridget Connor, GNSH and
Mary Fitzgerald, SSND

R Practicum Blueprint

outskirts
press

Credits

We acknowledge and thank the following people for their support, review, and feedback of Administration and Supervision documents:

Sister Sharon Slear, Dean School of Education

Advance Program Faculty/Staff, School of Education: Juliann Dupuis, Lisa Pallett, Carol Rabin, Joan Sattler, and Jeanette Quinn

Other Faculty/Staff: Ryan Schaff

Administrators/Mentor Administrators: Madeleine M. Hobik and Theresa A. Zablonski

Administration and Supervision Candidates/Graduates: David Ackley, Tonya Allen-Grier, Kristin Augenthaler, Daysha Baker, Kendra Banks, Daniel Brewer, Bradley Bauer, Jennifer Beach, James Blackwell, Jesse Braitman, Candice Cabezas, Diana Civera, Valerie Costantino, Heather Cucuzzella, Hillary Desir, Erin Divers, Lauren Grace, Ryan Harrigan, Katie Hauser, Jennifer Hayden, Kimberley Henein, Kristin Hilberg, Belinda Holmes, Shannon Karst, Caitlin Kincaid, Alyssa King, William Lewis, Christopher Matlack, Kelly Martin, Stacy Meadows, Despina Moniodis, Lauren Nehus, Renee Norona, Janine Paetow, Margaret Patrick, Jacqueline Paul, Nicole Pruet, Kara Riely, Jonathan Rogers, Rebecca Rogers, David Rosen, Hannah Ruckstuhl, Lauren Urban, Erica Sorg, Lauren Stefanovich, Kimberly Stevens Tracy Valentine

Table of Contents

Introduction

Welcome Candidate Administrators to a rich educational history envisioned by the School Sisters of Notre Dame (SSND). The College of Notre Dame of Maryland, now, Notre Dame of Maryland University (NDMU) was first chartered in 1896, the first Catholic College for women in the United States, in a time when higher education was not supported and rather discouraged for women. Social justice, therefore, education of women, has been a primary concern of SSND from their beginnings. The SSND founder, Mother Theresa, hoped to touch lives, to educate, to "trust and dare" and make this world a better place for all people. Today, many NDMU women and men, who dedicate their lives as educational leaders, continue the vision of the SSND, transforming the world in small and meaningful ways to foster God's reign of love and justice. We hope that your practicum experience is one that is meaningful and helpful in your development as a leader in the field of education.

The School of Education is nationally accredited and has been continuously approved by Maryland State Department of Education. Master of Arts in Leadership in Teaching was approved in 1992. Specialized core programs as the need required developed within the Master of Arts in Leadership and Teaching. The first track approved (1999) was the program for Administration and Supervision. The program in Administration and Supervision requires an onsite practicum intended to develop the knowledge, dispositions and skills needed for administrative positions. This program is carefully designed for those aspiring Administrator I certification by the Maryland State Department of Education.

A successful NDMU Candidate Administrator is required to know and act in accordance with professional standards, NDMU School of Education Outcome (SEO), the Professional Standards for Educational Leaders (PSEL), and the National Educational Leadership Preparation (NELP) Standards.

The program in Administration and Supervision in Notre Dame's School of Education requires that all successful candidates achieve the professional standards specified below:

- National Educational Leadership Preparation (NELP) Standards
- Professional Standards for Educational Leaders (PSEL)
- NDMU School of Educational Outcomes (SEO)
- Resources reflecting these standards can be found in the appendices.

The following practicum information will be helpful in planning the required on-site 300 hour administrative experience throughout Practicum I and Practicum II under the direction of an approved mentor administrator and university professor.

Candidate administrator's experiences are guided by an approved mentor administrator. It may be the principal of the school or his/her designee. It is essential to build a professional relationship with the mentor administrator. A successful practicum is dependent on the successful interaction of you, as the candidate, with your mentor administrator. NDMU has certain expectations of you, as candidate, in developing as a professional leader. Working closely with your mentor administrator will help to ensure a successful completion. The mentor administrator and your university professor will evaluate you on your ability to meet professional standards. Flexibility is a quality of a good administrator, adjusting for situations as needed. Respectful, and confidential interactions that reflect the highest of ethical decisions are expected of an educational professional.

Sister Sharon Slear, Dean of the School of Education, and visionary for this program would publically like to thank the mentor administrators.

A Letter to the Mentor-Administrator

Thank you for accepting our School Administration and Supervision candidate. We are very grateful to you for the wisdom you will share and the shadowing opportunities you will provide our candidate-administrator. The candidate will meet with you to discuss the requirements of the practicum, and to design the experience.

Expectations for the candidate, as well as suggested and required activities, are outlined in this booklet. Evaluation forms are included and we ask your cooperation in completing the evaluations at the end of each semester of the practicum experience.

If you have questions about the information in the booklet, your role as a mentor-administrator, or our program, please feel free to contact me at 410-532-3169 or sslear@ndm.edu.

Thank you for assisting us in preparing effective future administrators. Sincerely yours,

Sister Sharon Slear, SSND, Ph.D.

Dean of the School of Education, NDMU

Explanation of Practicum Experience

Notre Dame of Maryland University, School of Education, provides a two-semester experience for candidate administrators in Practicum I and Practicum II. This is an intensive experience in your local school setting with an approved mentor administrator. There are many assignments and task required over the course of your work but the following information is provided for you for your general understanding of the on-going nature of Practicum I and Practicum II. Over the period of Practicum I and Practicum II, 300 hours are required to be documented. Candidates are required to track their hours of administrative responsibilities in a time log. Practicum I (EDU 688) time log records minimally 100 hours of administrative duties. Practicum II records the remaining hours of the 300 required. The time logs are to be verified and signed by your mentor administrator.

The following are suggestions for administrative activities that could be included on the time log for Practicum I.

- Supervision
- Student arrival/departure Change of class Cafeteria
- Bus arrival/departure
- Shadowing an administrator for the day
- Participation in the School Improvement Team
- Organization, analyzing, and monitoring data for the team
- Monitoring and following up on attendance
- Arranging for substitutes
- Preparing professional development programs
- Attendance at School Board meetings
- Implementing the Change Project for the Practicum
- Involvement in Discipline Decisions
- Reviewing priorities of Budget
- Attendance of Parent Teacher Organization Meetings
- Writing curriculum with a team

- Rewriting Policy Handbook
- Filling in for an Assistant Principal in his/her absence
- Working on the school schedule
- Monitoring of After School Activities

Mentor-administrators may assign other meaningful administrative duties at their discretion

Time you take to do it & prepare it,

Time Record for Practicum Explanation

Candidate administrator (CA) is required to keep an accurate record of the time spent in various activities. The record should reflect the candidate's experiences in accord with the National Educational Leadership Preparation (NELP) Standards and Professional Standards for Educational Leaders (PSEL) and the School of Education Outcomes (SEO). This time log is best kept in Excel format which has a function for totaling hours.

Consistency is important in recording time. Time should be logged as fractions of an hour, e.g., 20 minutes = 20min/60min = 1/3 hour =.33 hour.

Time Log Template

Name: _____

Date	Hours	Description of Activity	NELP/PSEL Standards Met
Total Hours:			

Total Hours:

Mentor Administrator's Name: (Please print):

_____

Mentor Administrator's Signature:

_____

E-portfolio Artifact Requirements

Many of the assignments in Practicum I and Practicum II are required to be uploaded to an electric portfolio. At this point in your program you have been required to successfully upload and submit many assignments from different courses to your e-portfolio. E-portfolio questions can be addressed to Ryan Schaaf (rschaaf@ndm.edu). The following assignments are required to be uploaded and submitted to your professor.

Practicum I

EDU 688 E-Portfolio Requirements

1. Philosophy Statement
2. Leadership Vision and Change Project
3. Managing Resources: Examining the Budget
4. Mid-term Evaluation by Mentor Administrator

Practicum II

EDU 690 Required

1. Grade/Subject Level Involvement
2. Instructional Walkthrough
3. Global Policy
4. Collaboration with Families
5. Disciplinary Actions (Operations and Ethics)
6. Final Evaluation by Mentor Administrator
7. Leadership Exit Interview and Final PowerPoint Presentation

EDU 688

1. Leadership Philosophy Statement

Notre Dame of Maryland University is committed to preparing leaders who are compassionate and knowledgeable to serve in administrative roles and dedicated to providing the best possible educational environment for each student.

A leadership philosophy statement is what directs your interactions with others. The clearer that your leadership philosophy statement is to you, the more you will understand your interactions with others. Who you are, what you know, and how you use your knowledge to act, will greatly impact your leadership. In today's world of diversity and complexity, leadership roles demand a person who is rooted in integrity and social responsibility. In considering your leadership philosophy statement, carefully address

   a. Leadership Vision
   b. Personal and Professional Values that support differences (cultural, racial, exceptionalities, gender, etc.)
   c. Ethics that promotes moral and ethical behavior
   d. Supportive School Community
   e. Leadership Style

Philosophy Rubric

Criterion and Standards	Proficient (3)	Competent (2)	Developing (1)	Unacceptable (0)
Leadership Vision NELP 1.1 PSEL 1.a	Candidate's educational vision demonstrates clear and strong commitment to the success and well-being of all students and school personnel. Candidates	Candidate's educational vision demonstrates commitment to the success and well-being of all students and school personnel. Candidates can advocate	Candidate's educational vision demonstrates commitment to the success and well-being of all students but need to develop a clearer understanding of this	Candidate's philosophy statement does not give evidence of commitment to an educational vision.

Criterion and Standards	Proficient (3)	Competent (2)	Developing (1)	Unacceptable (0)
	can clearly advocate and implement the core elements of this vision.	advocate and implement the core elements of this vision.	commitment. Candidates demonstrate some ability to advocate and implement the core elements of this vision.	
Personal and Professional Values NELP 2.3 PSEL 3.a	His/her vision articulates a clear vision that strongly supports diversity, individual needs, exceptionalities and cultural differences.	His/her vision articulates a vision that supports diversity, individual needs, exceptionalities and cultural differences.	His/her vision articulates a vision that supports diversity, individual needs, exceptionalities and cultural differences. The statement needs further development.	Candidate did not clearly articulate support for diversity, individual needs and or cultural differences.
Ethics NELP 2.1 PSEL 2.f	Educational vision clearly articulates high ideals, integrity and ethical practices that promote right relationship, moral and professional behavior.	Educational vision articulates high ideals, integrity and ethical practices that promote right relationships, moral and professional behavior.	Educational vision articulates integrity and ethical practices that promote right relationships, moral and professional behavior. The statement needs further development.	Candidate's philosophy statement did not address expected professional ethical considerations.

Criterion and Standards	Proficient (3)	Competent (2)	Developing (1)	Unacceptable (0)
Supportive School Community NELP 3.4 PSEL 5.a	Philosophy statement clearly articulates a vision that will enhance a safe and quality educational environment where mutual respect and concern for individual needs and development are central.	Philosophy statement demonstrates a skill-based knowledge in providing an educational environment where mutual respect and concern for individual needs are central.	Philosophy statement demonstrates a skill-based knowledge but needs development in this area. Mutual respect and concern for individual needs are central but statement needs further development in this area.	Philosophy statement did not address expected areas.
Leadership Style NELP 7.3 PSEL 6.f	Statement clearly articulates the importance of collaboration that is inclusive of all stakeholders. Statement gives clear evidence of empowering teachers and staff to the highest level of professional performance.	Statement articulates the importance of collaboration that is inclusive of all stakeholders. Statement gives evidence of empowering teachers and staff to the highest level of professional performance.	Statement gives some evidence of acknowledging the importance of collaboration with stakeholders but needs further development. Statement gives some evidence of empowering teachers and staff to the highest level of professional performance but needs further development.	Statement does not sufficiently address collaboration and empowerment of appropriated stakeholders.

2. Leadership Vision and Change Project

Leadership Vision and Change Project is begun in Practicum I (688) but continued in Practicum II (690). Assignment instructions are detail here so that you can have a full understanding of what is expected throughout your internship. Adjustments may be needed to the project as directed by mentor administrator or because of other possible limitations.

The development of a Change Project is a major focus of Candidate Administrator's (CA) requirements for Practicum I (EDU 688). This project is to be sustained throughout the year and into Practicum II (EDU 690).

The project is identified through a collaborative process that is reflective of the school needs. Expectations:

1. CA is involved with the School Improvement Team (SIT) or its equivalent.
2. CA is to become familiar with the School Improvement Plan (SIP) (PSEL 1.e; NELP 1.1).
3. The candidate is responsible for identifying five of the greatest needs of the school and finally, in consultation with his/her mentor administrator, decides on one of those needs as the concern to address in the change project
4. CA is expected to analyze the existing problem, using relevant information from the school improvement plan or other sources, such as attendance records, demographics, school testing scores, MSDE report card, and other pertinent information that will have an impact on school climate and student learning. A general description of the proposed plan that is supported by research and best practices follows from the analyses of the problem (PSEL 1.b; NELP 1.1).
5. CA describes how this plan will affect the learning environment

through the use of the best practices proposed and effective management of resources. AC also addresses how this project will affect the overall school culture in meeting success (NELP 6.2; PSEL 9.c).

6. CA is to identify the key components of the mission/vision of the local school or district;
7. Articulate his/her own leadership vision;
8. Articulate his/her own vision for learners and teachers and finally
9. To describe the relationship that this proposed change project has to the school/district mission, including the impact that this project will have on the school culture, student learning and equality of education.

Working with a mentor administrator (NELP 8.3)), CA develops a change project that will clearly impact the school-learning environment. Permission from mentor administrator is required.

Additional Requirements Include:

1. Respectful and appropriate collaboration with faculty and community (PSEL 6.f ; NELP 7.2)
2. Acceptance of guidance in administrative activities
3. Attendance at School Improvement Team or equivalent
4. Conference with appropriate administrators in the planning stage and receive approval of project
5. Background information that clearly describes school, demographics, on-going problems, cultural differences, pertinent supportive data, and other significant information. This information will be essential in forming a rationale for the change project (NELP 3.2; PSEL 3.h)
6. A vision for learning influenced by school needs (NELP 1.4; PSEL 1.b)
7. Goals that are clear and measurable, inclusion of timeline and evaluative process (NELP 4.1; PSEL 4.a)
8. Rationale for the change project included data that analyzed existing problem/s

9. Inclusion of data and other information that drives improvement plan (NELP 4.3; PSEL 4.g)
10. A description of how this plan will be communicated
11. Clearly identified resources (personnel, finances and other) to complete plan (NELP 6.3; PSEL 9.b)
12. A description of how this plan will be implemented and evaluated for success (NELP 6.1; PSEL 9.a).
13. A vision that is based on sound research and current best pedagogical practices that is inclusive of national, state and local standards (NELP 4.2; PSEL 4.b)
14. Plan that is collaborative and includes faculty, community members and others in the planning and implementation (NELP 7.2; PSEL6.f)
15. Plan that involves the community, families and resources (NELP 5.3; PSEL 8.d)
16. 16. Plan that addresses the disadvantaged and provides equality of education (NELP 3.1; PSEL 3.c).

Leadership Vision and Change Project

Rubric

Criterion and Standards	Proficient (3)	Competent (2)	Developing (1)	Unacceptable (0)
Identification of School vision and development of leadership vision/ change project in keeping with school needs and plans NEEDS ASSESSMENT NELP 1.1 PSEL 1.b	Candidate administrator's "learning vision" or change project is directly and clearly related to the school improvement plan and school's mission for improved learning. The change project identifies the greatest needs of the school culture.	Candidate administrator's "learning vision" or change project is related to the school improvement plan. It reflects the school's mission for improved learning. The change project identifies the needs of the school.	Candidate administrator's "learning vision" or change project is related to the school improvement plan and reflects school's mission for learning. The change project is not strongly related to needs of school.	Candidate administrator's (CA)"learning vision" or change project does not adequately relate to the school improvement plan. It does not reflect the school's needs for improved learning.
DESIGN Includes: Rationale Understand root cause, analyze and advocate for students and families NELP 3.2 PSEL 3.h	Background information clearly described school, demographics, on- going problems, cultural differences, pertinent data and other	Background information described school, demographics, on-going problems, cultural differences, pertinent data and other significant	Background information described school, demographics, on-going problems, cultural differences, pertinent data as basis for project rationale	Background information did not adequately described school, demographics, on-going problems, cultural differences, pertinent data as basis

Criterion and Standards	Proficient (3)	Competent (2)	Developing (1)	Unacceptable (0)
	significant information as a basis for change project rationale	information as a basis for change project rationale		for project rationale
DESIGN Includes: Rationale that is researched based and includes use of data for academic improvement NELP 4.3 PSEL 4.g	CA's project is developed by using supportive data obtained from school improvement plan, its equivalent, MSDE report card, Benchmark tests, Standardized Testing (e.g.PARCC, IOWA) and other school records as appropriate. Goals for change project are clearly stated and measurable. A clear process is described as to how data will be used in the on- going process of plan development.	CA's project is developed by using data obtained from school improvement plan or its equivalent Goals for change project are stated and measurable. Process is described as to how data will be used in the on-going process of plan development.	CA's project is developed by using data obtained from school improvement plan or its equivalent Goals for change project are stated and measurable.	Goals are not adequately addressed AC did not describe adequate plans communicating goals and project.

Criterion and Standards	Proficient (3)	Competent (2)	Developing (1)	Unacceptable (0)
Leadership Vision: DESIGN and IMPLE-MENTATION Project is inclusive of faculty and school involvement NELP 7.2 PSEL 6.f	The plan demonstrates a highly effective collaborative model. Appropriate collaborators are actively involved in implementation of the change project.	The plan demonstrates a collaborative model. Appropriate collaborators are involved in the process.	The plan minimally demonstrates a collaborative model. Appropriate collaborators are minimally involved in the process.	The plan does not clearly involve others in planning or implementing the change project.
Leadership Vision: DESIGN and IMPLEMEN-TATION Project identifies Community Partners NELP 5.3 PSEL 8.d	Possible and strong community partners were identified.	Possible community partners were identified.	Community partners were superficially included in plan.	There were no community partners identified.
Leader Effective Management IMPLEMEN-TATION NELP 6.2 PSEL 9.c	CA plan, timeline, and identified resources demonstrate responsible, realistic and respectful involvement of school personnel, and community members that highly optimize his/her change project.	CA plan, timeline, and identified resources demonstrate responsible, realistic and respectful involvement of school personnel, and community members.	CA has created an adequate plan that demonstrates involvement of others.	CA has not sufficiently created a plan to implement the change project.

Criterion and Standards	Proficient (3)	Competent (2)	Developing (1)	Unacceptable (0)
EVALUATION and Assessment of Rigorous/ High Quality Project NELP 4.1 PSEL 4.a	CA has created a rigorous and comprehensive plan to implement the change project for school and student improvement	AC has created a comprehensive plan to implement the change project for school and student improvement	AC has created a an acceptable plan to implement the change project for school and student improvement	AC has not created an acceptable plan to implement the change project for school and student improvement
Parents and caregivers are partners in education. Partners are active members. Community members are involved NELP 5.2 PSEL 8.b	CA's plans include collaboration with families and community members as outlined in the change project and as recorded through process (email, phone calls, presentations, etc.)	CA's plans include collaboration with families and community members as outlined in the change project.	CA's plans minimally include collaboration with families and community members as outlined in the change project	CA's plans do not include collaboration with families and community members as outlined in the change project
Acts Fairly NELP 3.1 PSEL 3.c	CA's change project intentionally considers those at a disadvantage and plan reflects equality of education concerns.	CA's change project considers those at a disadvantage and plan reflects equality of education concerns.	CAs change project considers those at a disadvantage	CA's change project does not consider those at a disadvantage

Criterion and Standards	Proficient (3)	Competent (2)	Developing (1)	Unacceptable (0)
Monitor and evaluate operational systems. Evaluation and Assessment of High Quality Project Assessments are a regular part of ongoing evaluation NELP 6.1 PSEL 9.a	CA has established a clear time line, step by step plan, process for monitoring and taken initial steps for implementing change project	CA has established a time line, step by step plan, and process for monitoring.	CA has established a time line and process for monitoring.	CA has not established a time line, step by step plan, process for monitoring and taken initial steps for implementing change project
Mentor Administrator NELP 1.4 PSEL 1.b	In consultation with mentor administrator, other personnel, CA has clearly described the change project and has full support to move forward with change project or an alternate plan as devised with the needs of school and administrator. Timeline for project's implementation has been approved by mentor administrator and is comprehensively developed.	In consultation with mentor administrator, other personnel, CA has described the change project and has support to move forward with change project or an alternate plan as devised with the needs of school and administrator. Timeline for project's implementation has been approved by mentor administrator.	In consultation with mentor administrator, other personnel CA has described the change project and has support to move forward with change project or an alternate plan as devised with the needs of school and administrator. Timeline is not fully developed.	AC did not work with mentor administrator in an appropriate manner in developing change project

Leadership Vision and Change Project assignment is started in EDU 688 but continues in 690. Candidates are required to work with their mentor administrator and other stakeholders in the development and implementation of a change project that leads to overall success of the school's academic culture. This project was identified and planned in EDU 688 (Practicum I) and is sustained in EDU 690 (Practicum II). The evaluation of the Leadership Vision and Change Project is part of the Exit Interview and PowerPoint Presentation. The Exit Interview documents the continuance of the Change Project. Successes, revisions and challenges are reported at the exit interview.

3. Managing Resources: Examining the Budget

Task Description:

Examine the process by which the system-wide budget is constructed, proposed, approved and implemented (NELP 6.1; PSEL 9.a). Discuss the opportunities for local input, distribution of funds to your school, alignment with school improvement plan, and accountability of such funds with your administrator (NELP 6.2; PSEL 9.c). Identify the role of technology for increased efficiency in operations and management systems (NELP 6.3; PSEL 9.f). Using this information, provide a summary of learnings. Include a two to three page reflection describing the impact of this activity upon your perspective of administration.

Managing Resources: Examining the Budget Rubric

Criterion and Standard/s	Proficient (3)	Competent (2)	Developing (1)	Unacceptable (0)
Manage School Operations NELP 6.1 PSEL 9.a	Candidate's reflection clearly demonstrated knowledge of resources and fiscal planning.	Candidate's reflection demonstrated knowledge of resources and fiscal planning.	Candidate's reflection minimally demonstrated knowledge of resources and fiscal planning.	
Knowledge of economics and alignment of resources of operations and management to affect student learning NELP 6.2 PSEL 9.c	Candidate's reflection on operations and management clearly identified resources in alignment with student learning in a school	Candidate's reflection on operations and management identified resources in alignment with student learning in a school environment.	andidate's reflection on operations and management minimally identified resources in alignment with student learning in a school environment.	Candidate did not identify the alignment on operations and management items and student learning needs.

Criterion and Standard/s	Proficient (3)	Competent (2)	Developing (1)	Unacceptable (0)
	environment. Reflective statement comments on budget's priority of meeting student learning needs.	Reflective statement comments on budget's priority of meeting student learning needs.	*what if save?*	
Coordinate school management system inclusive of technology

NELP 6.3
PSEL 9.f | Candidate's reflection indicated clear understanding of best use of technologies for increased efficiency of operations and management systems | Candidate's reflection indicated understanding of use of technologies for increased efficiency of operations and management systems. | Candidate's reflection minimally demonstrated knowledge of technologies for increased efficiency of operations and management. | Candidate did not identify technologies for effective use in operations and management systems. |
| Grammar | Statement follows written standard English, free of errors in grammar, spelling, punctuation, and mechanics. There are no errors that impede meaning or distract the reader. | Statement follows standard written English with minimal errors in grammar, spelling, punctuation, and mechanics. Errors do not distract reader or impede meaning. | Statement follows standard written English with some errors in grammar, spelling, punctuation, and mechanics. Errors do not distract reader or impede meaning. | Statement includes errors in grammar, spelling, punctuation, and/or mechanics that impede the reader's ability to gain overall meaning |

Who does budget at school?
Have phone conversation - How is it done?
Use it to write paper.
Prepare & submit for approval?
to district.
Common budget template? Form? — Technology

21

4. Mid-term Evaluation by Mentor Administrator

Task Description

Candidates are required to work with a mentor administrator. They are required to fulfill administrative duties in a 300 hour time-frame in the total Practicum experience. Practicum I includes the first 100 to 150 hours.

Candidates have been involved in the School Improvement Team or its equivalent and interactive with administrative mentor (NELP 7.2; PSEL 7.c)).

They have identified a particular need of the school and have worked with their mentor teacher in creating a plan to address that need (NELP 1.1; PSEL 1.a).

This plan is a "learning vision" or change project that affects the school culture and student learning and addresses disparity within education (NELP 3.2; PSEL 3.c).

Candidates are required to describe their collaborative efforts in managing their plan. They are actively involved in instruction on consistent bases. They are expected to collaborate with subject grade partners or other curricular team members (NELP 6.3; PSEL 6.f). Candidate administrator clearly understand the use of assessment and data review for continued student progress (NELP 4.3; PSEL 4.g)

They are also expected to fulfill regular supervisory activities (NELP 6.1; PSEL 9.a).

They completed the budgetary assignment, noting alignment of priorities and student learning (NELP 6.2; PSEL 9.b).

Candidates demonstrate integrity and ethical conduct throughout their Practicum I experience (NELP 2.1; PSEL 2.a).

Mentor evaluation attests to candidate's abilities as a potential administrator.

Mid-Term Evaluation is based on the beginnings of administrative experiences (Practicum I). For that reason, score is based on those beginning experiences and expected potentials of the candidate. Print a copy of the evaluation form and give to your Mentoring Administrator.

Mid-Term Evaluation of Candidate-Administrator

Mentor-Administrator: _____

Candidate-Administrator: _____

Date: _____

Rubric Mid-Term Evaluation

Standard and Criterion	Proficient	Competent	Developing	Unacceptable
Professional Development Participate and respond to school and community interest NELP 7.2 PSEL 7.c	Candidate administrator attends the school improvement team or its equivalent. Candidate administrator is familiar with the School Improvement Plan or its equivalent. Candidate administrator has effectively communicated and connected with the mentor administrator.	Candidate administrator attends the school improvement team or its equivalent. Candidate administrator is familiar with the School Improvement Plan or its equivalent. Candidate administrator has effectively communicated and connected with the mentor administrator.	Candidate administrator attends the school improvement team or its equivalent. Candidate administrator is familiar with the School Improvement Plan or it's Equivalent. Candidate administrator has effectively communicated and connected with the mentor administrator.	Candidate administrator is not working with the school improvement team or plan (Or its equivalent). Candidate is not working effectively with mentor administrator.
Professional Development Collaborate, Develop, Articulate, Implement and Steward NELP 1.1 PSEL 1.a	Candidate administrator, after thoroughly reviewing school improvement plans and other documents and in collaboration with mentor administrator, plans on a change project that will clearly have an impact on school environment.	Candidate administrator, after reviewing school improvement plans and other documents and in collaboration with mentor administrator, plans on a change project that will have an impact on school environment.	Candidate administrator, after reviewing school improvement plans and other documents and in collaboration with mentor administrator, plans on a change project that will have an impact on school environment. Plans are not clearly developed.	Candidate administrator is not aware of school needs. He/she is not actively working with mentor administrator.

Standard and Criterion	Proficient	Competent	Developing	Unacceptable
Professional Development Promote school-based policies and procedure NELP 6.1 PSEL 9.a	Candidate reviewed and is keenly aware of school policies and procedures and is actively working with mentor administrator for effective school operations and management. This may include but not limited to cafeteria and bus monitoring, scheduling, and attending to after school or other student activities.	Candidate is aware of school policies and procedures and is actively working with mentor administrator for effective school operations and management. This may include but not limited to cafeteria and bus monitoring, scheduling, and attending to after school or other student activities.	Candidate is keenly aware of school policies and procedures and is actively working with mentor administrator for effective school operations and management. Candidate has, however, limited experience in activities, such as, cafeteria and bus monitoring, scheduling, and attending to after school or other student activities.	Candidate is not actively working with mentor administrator to develop skills in promoting school safety or welfare of students.
Professional Development Fiscal understanding and efficiency NELP 6.2 PSEL 9.b	Candidate has worked carefully and successfully with mentor administrator in understanding budgetary processes and alignment of resources to student learning needs.	Candidate has worked successfully with mentor administrator in understanding budgetary processes and alignment of resources to student learning needs.	Candidate is developing the skills necessary to work with mentor administrator in understanding budgetary processes and alignment of resources to student learning needs.	Candidate was not successful in working with the mentor administrator in completing the budget assignment

Standard and Criterion	Proficient	Competent	Developing	Unacceptable
Professional Development Collaboration as Instructional Leader NELP 6.3 PSEL 6.f	Candidate administrator is consistently working with team members on subject/ grade level planning and improvements for student success. .	Candidate administrator is working with team members on subject/ grade level planning and improvements for student success. .	Candidate administrator is working with team members on subject/ grade level planning and improvements for student success but not on consistent bases.	Candidate administrator does not show leadership abilities as an instructional leader.
Professional Development Assessment and data use NELP 4.3 PSEL 4.g	Candidate is very capable of using research-based strategies and clearly uses information to chart student progress. Candidate makes very good use of assessment information to disaggregate data to improve instruction.	Candidate is capable of using research-based strategies and clearly uses information to chart student progress Candidate makes use of assessment information to disaggregate data to improve instruction	Candidate is developing in his/her skills of using data for improvement of instruction.	Candidate does not demonstrate skills in using assessment for student learning.
Ethic/Integrity NELP 2.1 PSEL 2.a	Highly professional integrity, respect and interactive skills are demonstrated with faculty, staff and students.	Professional integrity, respect and interactive skills are demonstrated with faculty, staff and students.	Adequate respect and interactive skills are demonstrated with faculty, staff and students.	CA lacks interactive skills that are needed to work successfully with faculty, staff and students.

Standard and Criterion	Proficient	Competent	Developing	Unacceptable
Professional Development Personally Promote Social Justice NELP 3.2 PSEL 3.c	CA has clearly understood social justice and the equity principles and the change project have demonstrated the forwarding of these principles in a stellar manner.	CA has understood social justice and the equity principles and has competently forwarded these principles in the change project.	CA has adequate understanding of social justice and the equity principles and AC attempts to forward these principles.	CA does not concern him/herself with social justice and the equity principles and does not attempt to forward these principles.

Comments:

The following are assignments and required e-portfolio submission for EDU 690

1. Grade/Subject Level Involvement
2. Instructional Walkthrough
3. Global Policy
4. Collaboration with Families
5. Disciplinary Actions (Operations and Ethics)
6. Final Evaluation by Mentor Administrator
7. Leadership Exit Interview and Final PowerPoint Presentation

1. Grade/Subject Level Involvement

Administrative Candidates document their on-going involvement in instructional leadership (NELP 4.1; PSEL 4.a).

In a two to three-page report, describe your participation in grade/subject involvement and other committees that have helped to improve instructions in your school (NELP 4.1; PSEL 4.a). List any leadership initiatives that have improved instruction. Describe how attention is given to culturally responsive instruction and student diversity needs (NELP 3.2; PSEL 3.b).. Include in report the careful analyses of data that addresses any educational inequalities (NELP 3.3; PSEL 3.e). Include strengths and weaknesses of curricula to meet challenges for 21st century. If your curricular activities involve other areas of instructional oversight, please include those in your report.

Grade/Subject Level Involvements Rubric

Standards Criteria	Proficient (3)	Competent (2)	Developing (1)	Unacceptable (0)
Instructional Program with high expectations for students' success NELP 4.1 PSEL 4 a	Sustained involvement in instructional development and leadership initiative is described in detail.	Sustained involvement in instructional development is described in detail	Instructional development is explained in detail but reports lacks consistent evidence in instructional involvement.	Sustained involvement in instructional development is not demonstrated nor described in detail
Understand, create and evaluate curricular and instructional school program. NELP 3.2 PSEL 3.b	CA carefully and thoroughly detailed educational concerns, that included: Cultural responsive curricular instruction Diverse needs instruction Standard curricular alignment Student monitoring system	CA detailed educational concerns, that included: Cultural responsive curricular instruction Diverse needs instruction Standard curricular alignment Student monitoring system	CA minimally detailed educational concerns, such as: Cultural responsive curricular instruction Diverse needs instruction Standard curricular alignment Student monitoring system	CA did not sufficiently detail educational concerns.
Understand, collect and use data for effectiveness NELP 3.3 PSEL 3.e	CA made excellent use of formative and summative student data for improving results. Data was carefully analyzed for inequalities.	CA made use of formative and summative student data for improving results.	CA is developing the skills necessary to use student data for improving results.	CA does not show evidence for the use of student data for improving results.

2. Instructional Walkthrough

General Description

The purpose of this task is to help prepare you in your administrative responsibilities toward faculty. Working with your mentor administrator, you will be visiting and observing teachers in the process of instruction. As a candidate administrator, you are not allowed to formally make recommendations and any conversation or report developed for your mentor administrator is to be considered for the purpose of your personal growth as a potential administrator. Conversation and reports used for your learning process are also to be considered confidential. Use the list provided to select three focus areas for your data collection that are approved by your supervising administrator.

Number each teacher to be observed and list the number only on the form.

You should spend at least 10 minutes in at least 4 classrooms for each walk-through.

Record whether you observed the item or not and make any necessary notations.

A discussion of the process should occur following the walk-through with appropriate administrative personnel.

Write a reflection, briefly describing what you looked for, what you found in the classroom and the summary of the discussion that you had with the supervising administrator. Include how instructional time was or was not maximized for student learning (NELP 4.1; PSEL 4.a), an evaluation of the rigor of the instruction (NELP 4.2; PSEL 4.d), how the learning environment was conducive for student success and well being (NELP 3.2; PSEL 4.b). Identify leadership qualities in instructional practice (NELP 7.3; PSEL 7.b). List the commendation and recommendations for mentor administrator (NELP 7.2; PSEL 6.e).

Template: this may be done in Excel.

Teacher Number	Something that we all expect to see:	Item from generated from "Look For" lists	Item from generated from "Look For" list:	Notations:

Instructional Walk-Through

After a discussion with your supervising administrator, select at least three items from the following list to use to fill in the "Instructional Walk-through Chart." Record your observations on the chart in the appropriate column. After completing the Instructional Walk-Through and evaluation of observations have a follow up discussion with your mentor administrator

Instructional objectives that are:

Clearly posted.

Aligned to the standards for instruction.

Written in language that is understood by the teacher and students.

Reviewed before, during, and after instruction by teachers and students.

Instruction that:

Engages students and maximizes instructional time

Spans the levels of cognitive demand (i.e. literal, interpretive, and critical).

Supports and is aligned with the posted objective.

Includes time for teacher modeling, guided practice, and independent work.

Meets the individual learning needs of each student.

Daily formative assessment that:

Is aligned to the instructional objective.

Occurs at the conclusion of instruction.

Allows students to demonstrate their knowledge of the instructional objective as a result of the instruction.

Can be used by the teacher to inform instruction for the next lesson.

Can be used to provide appropriate feedback to assist students in improving future performance.

Instructional Walk-Through Rubric

Standards Criterion	Proficient (3)	Competent (2)	Developing (1)	Unacceptable (0)
High-quality instruction that maximizes instructional time NELP 4.1; PSEL 4.a	Candidate administrator's reflective statement clearly demonstrates his/her ability to keenly observe instructions that are of high-quality and that maximize instructional time. He/she clearly recognize effective and non-effective instructional strategies.	Candidate administrator's reflective statement demonstrates his/her ability to observe instructions that are of high-quality and that maximize instructional time. He/she recognize effective and non-effective instructional strategies.	Candidate administrator's reflective statement demonstrates a growing ability to observe instructions that is of quality and that maximizes instructional time.	Candidate is not able to demonstrate this awareness in his/her reflective statement
Instructional Program conducive to learning in personalized learning environment. NELP 4.2; PSEL 4.d	Candidate administrator's reflective statement clearly demonstrates an awareness of the best practice strategies that are conducive to student learning and that promote differentiated instruction and appropriate student interaction.	Candidate administrator's reflective statement demonstrates an awareness of the best practice strategies that are conducive to student learning and that promote differentiated instruction and appropriate student interaction.	Candidate administrator's reflective statement is developing an awareness of the best practice strategies that are conducive to student learning and that promote differentiated instruction and appropriate student interaction.	Candidate's reflective statement does not indicate awareness of the need for personalized learning

Standards Criterion	Proficient (3)	Competent (2)	Developing (1)	Unacceptable (0)
Develop School Leadership NELP 7.3 PSEL 7.b	CA's reflective statement clearly identified instructional leadership of particular faculty members and statement clearly reflects reason/s for this leadership.	CA's reflective statement identified instructional leadership of particular faculty members and statement reflects reason/s for this leadership.	CA's reflective statement identified instructional leadership of particular faculty members but reasons for such leadership were not fully described or comprehended.	CA's reflective statement did not reflect the identification of instructional leadership among faculty members.
Develop and Supervise Instructional Leadership NELP 3.2; PSEL 4.b	CA's reflective statement clearly demonstrates the ability to recognize key instructional concerns: lesson alignment to curriculum standards, objective/s and assessment,/s lesson alignment to diverse needs of students, and lesson engagement	CA's reflective statement demonstrates the ability to recognize key instructional concerns: lesson alignment to curriculum standards, objective /sand assessment/s, lesson alignment to diverse needs of students, and lesson engagement	CA's reflective statement demonstrates the ability to recognize some key instructional concerns: lesson alignment to curriculum standards, objective and assessment, lesson alignment to diverse needs of students, and lesson engagement	Candidate does not demonstrate acute awareness in these areas as noted on his/her reflective statement.
Evaluate for improved instruction NELP 7.2; PSEL 6.e	CA's reflective statement demonstrates his/her ability to provide highly effective alternatives to improve instructions	CA's reflective statement demonstrates his/her ability to provide effective alternatives to improve instructions.	CA's reflective statement demonstrates a growing ability to provide alternatives to improve instructions.	Candidate does not demonstrate acute awareness in these areas as noted on his/her reflective statement.

Standards Criterion	Proficient (3)	Competent (2)	Developing (1)	Unacceptable (0)
Format and Grammar	Statement follows written standard English, free of errors in grammar, spelling, punctuation, and mechanics. There are no errors that impede meaning or distract the reader.	Statement follows standard written English with minimal errors in grammar, spelling, punctuation, and mechanics. Errors do not distract reader or impede meaning.	Statement follows standard written English with some errors in grammar, spelling, punctuation, and mechanics. Errors do not distract reader or impede meaning.	Statement includes errors in grammar, spelling, punctuation, and/ or mechanics that impede the reader's ability to gain overall meaning

3. Managing Organization: Global Policy
EDU 690 SEO – Self-Reflection

Education That Is Multicultural

COMAR 13A.04.05.00

"Education that is multicultural prepares students to live, learn, interact, and work creatively in an interdependent global society by fostering mutual appreciation and respect."

The COMAR regulations are divided into three specific categories: a.) curriculum, b.) instruction, and c.) staff development. Each area is then divided into at least one goal and several objectives.

After reading the COMAR regulations below, select two of the three areas (Curriculum, Instruction, Staff Development) to use as a lens to examine your school. You will need to speak with your mentor-administrator and perhaps other grade level leaders or subject area leaders to learn what is done in your school in this regard (NELP 3.1; NELP 5.c).

Write a paragraph that analyzes what your school is or is not doing to address the objectives under each goal you have chosen that demonstrates your understanding of COMAR regulations (NELP 3.3; NELP 3.e). Reflective statement clearly indicates CA's understanding of regulation/s (NELP 6.4; PSEL 9.1). Statement reflects culture, context and diversity needed in instruction (NELP 3.2; PSEL 3.b). The law is binding and CA's reflection give evidence of this moral imperative (NELP 2.3 and PSEL 2.d).

Write a concluding paragraph that explains how addressing the goals and objectives above will prepare your students to meet the demands of life in a global society (NELP 7.2; NELP 3.f)

13A.04.05.00

Title 13A STATE BOARD OF EDUCATION

Subtitle 04 SPECIFIC SUBJECTS

Chapter 05 Education that is Multicultural

Authority: Education Article, §2-205(c) and (h), Annotated Code of Maryland

.04 Goals.

A. Curriculum.

(1) Goal. To provide Pre-K—12 curriculum, which enables students to demonstrate an understanding of and an appreciation for cultural groups in the United States as an integral part of education for a culturally pluralistic society. The curriculum shall enable students to apply these skills to fully participate in the democratic process of their community, State, nation, and world. The curriculum includes the following content:

(a) Emphasis on correcting the omissions and misrepresentations of African Americans, Asian Americans, Latinos, Native Americans, women, and individuals with disabilities;

(b) The history of cultural groups and their contributions in Maryland, in the United States, and in the world;

(c) Historic events, situations, conflicts, and interpretations from diverse perspectives;

(d) Political, social, and economic conditions which cultural groups have experienced and continue to experience in the United States; and

(e) As appropriate, issues of racism, sexism, bias, and prejudice as these affect the behavior and experience of individuals and groups.

(2) Goal. To provide Pre-K—12 curriculum, which develops the valuing of cultural groups in the United States as an integral part of education for a culturally pluralistic society. The curriculum shall provide opportunity for students to demonstrate the following attitudes and actions:

(a) Valuing one's heritage;

(b) Valuing the uniqueness of cultures other than one's own;

(c) Valuing the richness of cultural diversity and commonality;

(d) Respecting diverse cultural groups throughout the world;

(e) Awareness of and sensitivity to individual differences within various cultural groups;

and

(f) Eliminating stereotypes related to race, ethnicity, region, religion, gender, socioeconomic status, age, and individuals with disabilities.

B. Instruction.

(1) Goal. To provide Pre-K—12 instruction which will enable students to develop an understanding of and appreciation for cultural groups as an integral part of education for a culturally pluralistic society (NELP 3.2; PSEL 3.b).

(2) The instructional program shall:

(a) Promote a school climate that reflects the diversity of the community;

(b) Promote a school climate in which different cultural linguistic patterns are respected;

(c) Promote grouping of students to reflect cultural diversity;

(d) Ensure that a student may not be denied access to equally rigorous academic instruction on the basis of cultural background;

(e) Use instructional activities which recognize and appreciate students' cultural identities and learning styles;

(f) Address racism, sexism, bias, discrimination, and prejudice;

(g) Use organizations promoting cultural and ethnic understanding;

(h) Use instructional activities that promote an understanding of and a respect for a variety of ways of communicating, both verbal and nonverbal;

(i) Use instructional materials which reinforce the concept of the United States as a pluralistic society within a globally interdependent world while recognizing our common ground as a nation;

(j) Incorporate multicultural instructional materials in all subject areas; and

(k) Provide opportunities for students to analyze and evaluate social issues and propose solutions to contemporary social problems.

C. Staff Development.

(1) Goal. To include in staff development experiences that prepare school system personnel to design, manage, implement, and evaluate multicultural education.

(2) The experiences in §D (1) of this regulation includes:

(a) Activities which involve professional and support staff in exploring attitudes and feelings about their own cultural identity;

(b) Activities to identify instructional strategies, techniques, and materials appropriate for education that is multicultural;

(c) Training in assessing the prior knowledge, attitudes, abilities, and learning styles of students from varied backgrounds in order to develop multicultural instructional programs;

(d) Training to recognize and correct stereotyping, discrimination, bias, and prejudice;

(e) Training for fostering greater intergroup understanding;

(f) Training to recognize and correct the omissions and misrepresentations of groups and individuals in curriculum and instruction;

(g) Training to recognize and correct inequitable participation in school activities by students and staff from different backgrounds; and

(h) Training to identify human resources for education that is multicultural.

Global Policy Rubric

Criterion Standard/s	Proficient (3)	Competent (2)	Developing (1)	Unacceptable (0)
Understand and Promote school-based policies and procedures and support systems that protect the welfare of students NELP 3.1; PSEL 5.c	Candidate's reflective statement gives evidence of clear understanding of COMAR regulations and the importance of these regulations for students' well-being inclusive of culture and context.	Candidate's reflective statement gives evidence of understanding of COMAR regulations and the importance of these regulations for students' well-being inclusive of culture and context.	Candidate's reflective statement is developing in the understanding of COMAR regulations and the importance of these regulations for students' well-being inclusive of culture and context.	Candidate did not demonstrate sufficient understanding and implication of COMAR regulations.
Understand and promote cultural, social and intellectual differences NELP 3.2 PSEL 3.b	Candidate's reflective statement gives clear evidence of knowledge and strong support for diverse cultural, social and intellectual needs of students	Candidate's reflective statement gives evidence of knowledge and support for diverse cultural, social and intellectual needs of students.	Candidate's reflective statement gives evidence of knowledge and support for diverse cultural, social and intellectual needs of students but statement needs further development.	Candidate's reflective statement does not give evidence of the diverse cultural, social and intellectual needs of students.

Criterion Standard/s	Proficient (3)	Competent (2)	Developing (1)	Unacceptable (0)
Moral and Legal Obligation NELP 2.3 PSEL 2.d	Candidate's statement clearly reflects that he/she will comply with regulations of COMAR and considers it his/her moral obligation.	Candidate's statement reflects that he/she will comply with regulations of COMAR and considers it his/her moral obligation.	Candidate's statement reflects the need for compliance to COMAR regulations but needs further development.	Candidate's statement does not reflect the importance COMAR regulations.
Social Justice equitable education and disparities NELP 3.3; PSEL 3.e	Candidate's reflective statement clearly describes the connection of student diversity and social justice in providing equitable education. CA's reflection recognizes any deficit or inequalities.	Candidate's reflective statement describes the connection of student diversity and social justice in providing equitable education. CA's reflection recognizes deficit or inequalities.	Candidate's reflective statement is developing in the ability to describe the connection of student diversity and social justice in providing equitable education.	Candidate's reflective statement has not connected the concept of student diversity and social justice in providing equitable education.
Understands laws, policies and regulations NELP 6.4 PSEL 9.1	Candidate clearly understands COMAR regulations and how it affects the school. The written explanation specifically addresses all objectives relating to the two selected goals.	Candidate understands COMAR regulations and how it affects the school. The written explanation addresses all objectives relating to the two selected goals.	Candidate is developing in the understanding of COMAR regulations and how it affects the school. The written explanation addresses some of the objectives relating to the two selected goals.	Candidate did not meet expectations.

Criterion Standard/s	Proficient (3)	Competent (2)	Developing (1)	Unacceptable (0)
Understand policies and laws and student development for global society NELP 7.2; PSEL 3.f	The concluding paragraph thoroughly explains how the objectives relate to life in a global society and the impact of COMAR directives for student learning.	The concluding paragraph explains how the objectives relate to life in a global society and the impact of COMAR directives for student learning.	The concluding paragraph minimally explains how the objectives relate to life in a global society and the impact of COMAR directives for student learning.	Candidate administrator does not understand or explain the objectives and relationship to the global society.
Grammar	Statement follows written standard English, free of errors in grammar, spelling, punctuation, and mechanics. There are no errors that impede meaning or distract the reader.	Statement follows standard written English with minimal errors in grammar, spelling, punctuation, and mechanics. Errors do not distract reader or impede meaning.	Statement follows standard written English with some errors in grammar, spelling, punctuation, and mechanics. Errors do not distract reader or impede meaning.	Statement includes errors in grammar, spelling, punctuation, and/ or mechanics that impede the reader's ability to gain overall meaning

4. Collaborating with Families: Effective Conferences (EDU 690) SEO – Self-Reflection

Task Description:

Solicit feedback from parents and teachers on factors that contribute to effective conferences (NELP 5.1; PSEL 8.b).

Examine relevant research for the same.

Discuss the findings with your administrator.

Using this information, document your role in developing and disseminating successful conference strategies. Include a reflection describing the impact of this activity upon your perspective of administration.

Collaborating with Families Rubric

Criterion and Standard	Proficient	Competent	Developing	Unacceptable
Building Positive School Relationships with Families and Caregivers NELP 5.1 PSEL 8.b	Documentation provided a thorough indication of the candidate's active involvement in presenting successful conference strategies to stakeholders. Reflection was insightful, and future-oriented	Documentation provided adequate indication of the candidate's involvement in presenting successful conference strategies to stakeholders. Reflection was clearly stated and had future direction.	Documentation provided minimal indication of the candidate's involvement in presenting successful conference strategies to stakeholders. Reflection was clearly stated but lacked future direction.	Documentation did not provide adequate involvement or strategies.
Grammar	Statement follows written standard English, free of errors in grammar, spelling, punctuation, and mechanics. There are no errors that impede meaning or distract the reader.	Statement follows standard written English with minimal errors in grammar, spelling, punctuation, and mechanics. Errors do not distract reader or impede meaning.	Statement follows standard written English with some errors in grammar, spelling, punctuation, and mechanics. Errors do not distract reader or impede meaning.	Statement includes errors in grammar, spelling, punctuation, and/or mechanics that impede the reader's ability to gain overall meaning

5. Disciplinary Actions: Operations and Ethics (EDU 690 SEO – Vocation)
Description of School Culture

Discipline Action: Operations /Models Integrity and Fairness

Part 1

Operations: As a candidate administrator, your responsibilities include managing overall safe environment that promotes healthy relationships and effective learning environment (NELP 2.3, PSEL 3.d). Understanding the culture and responding appropriately, responsibly and ethically are required of a professional administrator (NELP 3.1, PSEL 3.a).

Describe the school culture and use of information to complete a concise "School Culture Report" (NELP 3.4; PSEL 1.c).

In the report, include school's records of detention, suspension and absenteeism. Record statistical data in a table format. Include other data if available (NELP 6.2 PSEL 9.g).

In the report, describe school discipline policy and school-wide discipline plan (NELP 6.4; PSEL 9.h)..

Describe its effectiveness or lack of effectiveness.

What changes might you make to improve it? Describe your responsibility as an administrator in the developing of a positive school environment. How do you act as a model for teachers and students?

Part 2

Disciplinary Actions:

Described three discipline cases in which you were involved.

Describe how the management of these cases assisted in effective operations and student growth (NELP 2.1; PSEL 2.a).

How have these experiences impacted you as a perspective administrator?

Part 3

Use the three case studies from Discipline Involvement: Actions. This may be done in essay format or by using a chart like the one below.

Describe the background, setting, the problem and your personal involvement

(NELP 2.4; PSEL 2.f).

Describe how your actions were in keeping with laws and policies of fairness and how this is connected to your personal and professional code of ethics (PSEL 9.h).

What was your administrative responsibility and were you satisfied with your actions (NELP 2.2; PSEL 2.b) Evaluation).

Part 1. Description of school culture	School's discipline policy and school-wide discipline plan	Data: School's records pf detention, suspension, and absenteeism
What changes to school culture would you make to improve it?	Describe effectiveness or lack of effectiveness of policies and plans	Describe your responsibilities as candidate administrator in developing school environment.
Part2 Discipline Cases		
Description of Three Experience Regarding Discipline	Reflection on Experience	Possible Future Implications Due to Experience
1.		
2.		
3.		
Part 3 Reflection of Candidate Administrator responsibilities and actions taken in light of fairness and integrity.	Connect your actions to your personal and professional code of ethics.	What changes in your actions might you take?

School Culture, Discipline and Ethics Rubric

Criterion and Standards	Proficient 3	Competent 2	Developing 1	Unacceptable 0
Manage the Organization Culture/ Context NELP 3.1 PSEL 3.a	School culture report included a clear description of culture and discipline policy. Report clearly described school-wide discipline plan and its effectiveness or lack of effectiveness.	Report included data, description of culture and discipline policy. Report described school-wide discipline plan and its effectiveness or lack of effectiveness.	Report included minimal data. Description of discipline policy is clear. Report on school-wide discipline plan lack detailed.	CA did not describe in detail expected school policies.
Use of Data/ Support NELP 6.2 PSEL 9.g	School culture report included detailed data and these data were clearly used to support statements.	School culture report included data and these data were used to support statements.	School culture report minimally included data and these data were used to support statements.	No data were used to support school culture report.
Support School Culture and Community NELP 3.4 PSEL 1.c	Administrative actions are in keeping with school policies. Decisions and actions ensure utmost respect towards all involved.	Administrative actions are in keeping with school policies. Decisions and actions ensure respect towards all involved.	CA managed disciplinary situation in keeping with school policies but had some difficulties in doing so.	CA does not ensure proper respect or student responsibility.
Values/ Discipline and Safety NELP 2.3 PSEL 3.d	Safety is a primary consideration in decision-making. Decisions and consequences encouraged student growth, healthy relationships, and responsibility	Safety was considered in decision-making. Decisions and consequences encouraged student, healthy relationships and responsibility.	Safety was considered in decision-making. Decisions and consequences support student responsibility but statement needs further development.	Safety was not considered. Decisions and consequences did not encourage student responsibility.

Criterion and Standards	Proficient 3	Competent 2	Developing 1	Unacceptable 0
Fairness NELP 2.1 PSEL 2.a	Management of discipline case applied laws and procedures fairly, wisely and considerately. Student and all involved were treated fairly, equitably and with dignity and respect.	Management of discipline case applied laws and procedures fairly. Student and all involved were treated fairly and equitably.	Student and all involved were treated fairly and equitably.	Description is nebulous about fairness issues.
Ethical NELP 2.4 PSEL 2.f	Insightfully examined personal and professional values. Demonstrated personal and professional code of ethics.	Examined personal and professional values. Demonstrated personal and professional code of ethics.	Examined personal and professional values. Lacking in clear statement of ethics.	Lacking in personal value statements.
Evaluate Decision-Making NELP 2.2 PSEL 2.b	Candidate's reflective statements clearly bespeak of integrity. CA reflectively and creatively incorporated experiences for personal administrative growth	Candidate's reflective statements are indicative of integrity. CA reflectively incorporated experiences for personal administrative growth.	Candidate's reflective statements are minimally indicative of integrity. CA indicated little reflection for personal administrative growth.	Candidates did not reflect for personal growth as an administrator.

Criterion and Standards	Proficient 3	Competent 2	Developing 1	Unacceptable 0
Grammar	Statement follows written standard English, free of errors in grammar, spelling, punctuation, and mechanics. There are no errors that impede meaning or distract the reader.	Statement follows standard written English with minimal errors in grammar, spelling, punctuation, and mechanics. Errors do not distract reader or impede meaning.	Statement follows standard written English with some errors in grammar, spelling, punctuation, and mechanics. Errors do not distract reader or impede meaning.	Statement includes errors in grammar, spelling, punctuation, and/or mechanics that impede the reader's ability to gain overall meaning

6. Final Mentor Administrator Evaluation of Candidate Administrator-Practicum II SEO - Practice

Assigned mentor administrator has been working with the candidate administrator throughout his/her internship. Required artifacts are uploaded to an e-portfolio and are recorded. Mentor administrator work closely with the candidate administrator assisting in a successful experience. At the end of the internship, a mentor administrator completes this final form and candidate administrators are to give a hard copy to university supervisor and either type score on another copy and upload or scan document and upload. This document is sent to university supervisor for final confirmation.

Task Description

Over the course of two semesters, candidate administrators complete a 300-hour internship (NELP 8.1). The internship is within a local setting; candidates are required to fulfill administrative duties and record activities in log (NELP 8.2). The 300-hour internship is verified by mentor administrator and submitted to university supervisor (NELP 8.3). Candidates are required in artifact form, and in his/her time log to give evidence for:

- Attendance at School Board, Administrative, Faculty, School Improvement Team meetings, and other professional activities
- Administrative duties, bus evacuation exercises, discipline cases, budgetary involvement, and other daily duties
- Participation in grade/subject involvement -analyzing data/revising instructional strategies (NELP 6.2; PSEL 4.g)
- Progress on vision/change project (NELP 1.4; PSEL 1.b)
- Participation in scheduling and duties for increasing effective and efficient learning environment (NELP 4.1; PSEL 4.a)
- Completion of faculty/staff Technology Survey and report (NELP 4.4; PSEL 4.e)
- Parent/faculty/community Communication(collaboration) Chart included record of email, phone conversations, letters, and other contacts
- Completion of discipline cases addressing ethical (NELP 2.4; PSEL 2.a) and operational concerns (NELP 6.1; PSEL 9.a)
- Examination of the Budget
- Review of laws, policies, school handbooks and implements (NELP 5.4; PSEL 9.h)
- Required meetings (School Board, PTA, Administrative, School Improvement Team meetings) were recorded in time log (NELP 6.4; PSEL 9.l)
- Completion of informal teacher observations and report (NELP 7.4; PSEL 6.e)
- Evidence of successful faculty/staff/parents/ students interactions (NELP 3.4; PSEL 7.d)
- Participate in review, evaluation data, monitoring and recommending changes for student learning (NELP 6.2; PSEL 4.g)
- Advances equality of education and addressing inequalities through change project (NELP 2.3; PSEL 2.d)
- Participative leadership in developing trusting relationship and positive school culture (NELP 3.4; PSEL 7.c)

- Use of current and research-based strategies, required assessments for student success NELP 4.3; PSEL 4.b)
- Demonstrates professional integrity, fairness and mutual respect with all stakeholders NELP 2.1; PSEL 2.b)
- Other duties as requested

While each of these artifacts are uploaded to an e-portfolio, submitted to university supervisor, and scored individually, the mentor administrator, in a summative evaluation, reviews the candidate administrator's work over the internship. Mentor evaluation attests to candidate's abilities as a potential administrator.

Final Mentor Evaluation of Candidate-Administrator

Administration and Supervision

Mentor-Administrator: _____

Candidate-Administrator: _____

Date: _____

Criterion and Standards	Proficient (3)	Competent (2)	Developing (1)	Unacceptable (0)
Vision NELP 1.4 PSEL 1.b	Candidate Administrator (CA) worked professionally and cooperatively with assigned Mentor Administrator (MA). Together, CA and MA, using all available information and in keeping with school needs and improvement plan/s developed a needed change project. CA successfully directed the project to its conclusion, revising as required.	Candidate Administrator (CA) worked cooperatively with assigned Mentor Administrator (MA). Together, CA and MA, using available information and in keeping with school needs and improvement plan/s developed a needed change project. CA directed the project to its conclusion.	Candidate Administrator (CA) worked cooperatively with assigned Mentor Administrator (MA). Together, CA and MA, using available information developed a needed change project. CA minimally directed the project to its conclusion.	Candidate Administrator was not able to work with Mentor Administrator in developing a change project as required.
Instructional Program NELP 6.2 PSEL 4.g	CA participated fully in curricular team/s efforts in analyzing data and instructional program for the improvement of student achievement. This was reported in grade/subject level involvement or other appropriate method. CA	CA participated in curricular team effects in analyzing data and instructional program for the improvement of student achievement. This was reported in grade/subject level involvement or other appropriate method.	CA minimally participated in curricular team effects in analyzing data and instructional program for the improvement of student achievement. This was reported in grade/subject level involvement or other appropriate method.	CA did not give evidence of on-going analysis of data and review of instructional programs for improvement of student achievement

Criterion and Standards	Proficient (3)	Competent (2)	Developing (1)	Unacceptable (0)
	kept MA fully aware of this on-going work.			
Develop and supervise instructional leadership NELP 7.4 PSEL 6.e	CA clearly demonstrated skills necessary for supervision as evidenced in required observations, curricular decisions and other daily administrative duties.	CA sufficiently demonstrated skills necessary for supervision as evidenced in required observations, curricular decisions and other daily administrative duties.	CA had some difficulty in demonstrating skills necessary for supervision as evidenced in required observations and other daily administrative duties.	CA did not demonstrate skills necessary for supervision.
Promote and support technologies for teaching and learning NELP 4.4 PSEL 4.e	CA completed required faculty/staff technology survey indicating priorities and resources needed. The report was comprehensive and reviewed by mentor administrator and submitted to professor as required.	CA completed required faculty/staff technology survey indicating priorities and resources needed. The report was acceptable and reviewed by mentor administrator. Report was submitted to professor as required.	CA completed required faculty/staff technology survey indicating priorities and resources needed. The report was lacking details. Report was submitted to professor as required.	CA did not complete required survey.

Criterion and Standards	Proficient (3)	Competent (2)	Developing (1)	Unacceptable (0)
Sustained School Improvement NELP 8.1	Candidate's required 300 hours of administrative internship was met within the required school building in an effective and efficient manner. Time was used effectively for advancement of learning environment.	Candidate's required 300 hours of administrative internship was very closely met within the required school building in an effective manner. Time was used effectively for advancement of learning environment.	Candidate's required 300 hours of administrative internship was implemented in required school building and was no less than 275 hours.	Hours were not met.
Mentor Administrator Signature Internship NELP 8.3	Internship log was submitted with signature of mentor administrator and submitted to university supervisor in a timely fashion.	Internship log was submitted with signature of mentor administrator and submitted to university supervisor in a timely fashion.	Internship log was submitted with signature of mentor administrator and submitted to university supervisor in a timely fashion.	Internship log was not submitted
High quality school instruction NELP 4.1 PSEL 4.a	CA consistently and appropriately involved others in high quality plans to improve student learning Schedules are efficient and effective. This is evidenced in grade/subject level involvement, change project and daily school routines	CA appropriately involved others in quality plans to improve student learning Schedules are effective. This is evidenced in grade/subject level involvement, change project and daily school.	CA adequately involved others in plans to improve student learning Schedules are effective. This is evidenced in grade/subject level involvement, change project and daily school.	CA has not demonstrated the skills necessary for the development and implementation of high quality instruction for students.

Criterion and Standards	Proficient (3)	Competent (2)	Developing (1)	Unacceptable (0)
Participation is quality instructional program through trusting, collaborative and respectful interactions NELP 3.4 PSEL 7.c	CA encourages a positive school culture where learning is highly valued. This has been demonstrated by strong instructional leadership and the respectful relationships with faculty/ staff/parents/ students that have been maintained throughout internship.	CA encourages a positive school culture where learning is valued. This has been demonstrated by instructional leadership and the respectful relationships with faculty/ staff/parents/ students that have been established during the internship.	Instructional leadership skills and working relationships needed for administration are developing but not maintained.	CA does not clearly support a positive school culture where learning is valued and personnel are respected.

Criterion and Standards	Proficient (3)	Competent (2)	Developing (1)	Unacceptable (0)
Evaluate and revise school progress NELP 4.3 PSEL 4.b	Candidate is very capable of using research based strategies and clearly uses information to chart student progress. Candidate makes use of Maryland' Report Card site and/or other appropriate data. Candidate knows how and uses disaggregate data to improve instruction. Candidate is clearly aware and makes good use of formative and summative assessments for student learning.	Candidate competently uses research based strategies and clearly uses information to chart student progress. Candidate makes use of Maryland' Report Card site and uses disaggregate data to improve instruction. Candidate is aware and makes good use of formative and summative assessments for student learning.	Candidate adequately uses research based strategies and clearly uses information to chart student progress. Candidate makes use of Maryland' Report Card site. Candidate is aware and makes good use of formative and summative assessments for student learning.	Candidate does not demonstrate skills in using assessment for student learning.
Self-reflective/ ethical behavior NELP 2.4 PSEL 2.a	Candidate has willingly accepted supervisory activities suggested by mentor administrator. He/she has participated in administrative task including discipline concerns	Candidate has willingly accepted supervisory activities suggested by mentor administrator. He/she has participated in administrative task including discipline concerns	Candidate has accepted supervisory activities suggested by mentor administrator. He/she has participated in administrative task including discipline concerns	Candidate has not demonstrated the professional and ethical skills needed for an administrator.

Criterion and Standards	Proficient (3)	Competent (2)	Developing (1)	Unacceptable (0)
	and other daily operations of the school in a highly ethical, professional and legal manner.	and other daily operations of the school in an ethical, professional and legal manner.	and other daily operations of the school in an ethical, professional and legal manner.	
Advocate NELP 5.4 PSEL 9.h	Candidate has reviewed educational laws, policies, school regulations, and handbook as expected and consistently implements these laws and requirements to ensure equity of education.	Candidate has reviewed educational laws, policies, school regulations, and handbook as expected and implements these laws and requirements to ensure equity of education.	Candidate has reviewed educational laws, policies, school regulations, handbook as expected but needs further experience for full understanding and implementation.	Candidate does not show sufficient knowledge of educational laws and regulations.
Knowledge to Influence Knowledge for results in school improvement NELP 6.4 PSEL 9.l	CA has attended School Board, School Improvement, Administrative, Faculty, PTA meetings and is aware of the larger political, social, economic, legal and cultural concerns and has the ability to act on this information on the behalf of students. Required time	CA has sufficient attendance at School Board, School Improvement, Administrative, Faculty, PTA meetings and is aware of the larger political, social, economic, legal and cultural concerns and has the ability to act on this information on the behalf of students. Required time log	CA has attended School Board, School Improvement, Administrative, Faculty, PTA meetings and has some awareness of the larger political, social, economic, legal and cultural concerns. Required time log minimally give evidence to attendance at meetings of the	CA has not shown initiative in attendance at needed meetings for the understanding required of administrators.

Criterion and Standards	Proficient (3)	Competent (2)	Developing (1)	Unacceptable (0)
	log gives ample evidence of attendance and involvement at such meetings.	gives evidence of attendance and involvement at such meetings.	broader community.	
Monitor and evaluate operational systems NELP 6.1 PSEL 9.a	CA has demonstrated excellence in managing daily operations including the successful work with student discipline.	CA has demonstrated the abilities in managing daily operations including the successful work with student discipline.	CA has demonstrated some abilities in managing daily operations including the successful work with student discipline.	CA has not demonstrated the skills needed for successful management of operations
Integrity and fairness Mutual respect NELP 2.1 PSEL 2.b	Professional integrity, respect and positive interactive skills are demonstrated to an outstanding degree in dealings with faculty, staff and students.	Professional integrity, respect and interactive skills are demonstrated with faculty, staff and students.	Adequate- interactive skills are demonstrated with faculty, staff and students. Development in this area is needed.	CA lacks interactive skills that are needed to work successfully with faculty, staff and students.
Social Justice in addressing student needs NELP 2.3 PSEL 2.d	CA has clearly understood social justice and the equity principles and the change project have demonstrated the forwarding of these principles in a stellar manner.	CA has understood social justice and the equity principles and the change project have demonstrated the forwarding of these principles in a competent manner.	CA has adequate understanding of social justice and the equity principles and CA attempts to forward these principles.	CA does not concern him/herself with social justice and the equity principles and does not attempt to forward these principles.

Criterion and Standards	Proficient (3)	Competent (2)	Developing (1)	Unacceptable (0)
Sustained NELP 8.2	AC displays exceptional leadership and professionalism. AC accepts the proper responsibility. He/she has the ability to make timely and appropriate decisions. CA exceptionally fulfilled the requirements of a year-long internship	CA displays leadership and professionalism. AC accepts responsibility. He/she has the ability to make appropriate decisions. CA fulfilled the requirements of a year-long internship	CA has the potential for leadership with further experience necessary. CA accepts responsibility, and is decisive when necessary. CA has adequately fulfilled the requirements of a year-long internship.	CA does not exemplify the professional qualities necessary for administration. CA has not fulfilled required year-long internship.

Comments:

7. Leadership Exit Interview and Final PowerPoint Presentation

Final Presentation GEDU 690

General Directions

BE on time for your appointment. Leave your school or home early to be certain you are not held up in traffic.

Be professionally dressed: Gentlemen – shirt, tie, jacket, with pants; Ladies – dress slacks or skirt with appropriate blouse, an appropriate dress, or suit.

Greet the professors.

Introduce yourself and tell where you work and what your role is in your school.

Give each professor present a hard copy of your PowerPoint.

Give a brief background of your school.

Address the NELP and PSEL standards and your achievement of them by telling of administrative duties which you performed.

Give the rationale for the change project which you did.

Give an update on the progress of the change project.

Verify that you have completed 300 hours in the internship (NELP 8.1). BRING A COPY OF YOUR TIME LOG TO PRESENT TO PROFESSOR.

Identify at least one area in which you would like further professional growth (NELP 7.3; PSEL 6.h).

FOR YOUR PRESENTATION:

USE CORRECT LANGUAGE

USE APPROPRIATE PROFESSIONAL TERMINOLOGY

You have 20 minutes to present. You may use index cards to keep yourself focused.

University Professor will complete this form at your final presentation. CAs are expected to upload this document to their e-portfolio.

Task Description

Candidates' final Exit Interview and PowerPoint Presentation include the clear involvement and explanation of that involvement of candidate's internship throughout the year. The required 300 hours of internship work (NELP 8.1) is documented and explained in this session. The exit interview and PowerPoint Presentation demonstrates the candidate administrator's growth over the year as he/she has practiced and reflected on the professional responsibilities of forwarding school core values and mission (NELP 1.2; PSEL 1.g). Candidate demonstrates his/her direct and indirect involvement in duties of administrator by attendance at school board, school improvement team, administrative and faculty meetings (NELP 1.3; PSEL 1.d). Presentation includes an explanation of leadership involvement and communication that the candidate has in curricula development and daily supervisory activities of the school (NELP 6.3; PSEL 7.e). He/she gives evidence of parent/guardian/family communication (NELP 5.1; PSEL 8.c). The candidate explains his/her subject/grade involvement. Specifically, the candidate explains his/her sustained work in curricular meetings and development for continued student progress (NELP 1.4; PSEL 1.e)). Review of content standards, report of change project, analysis of student learning, revisions and interventions are part of an on-going process (NELP 3.3;PSEL 1.g). The candidate's presentation clearly describes daily management of school operations. The candidate describes his/her involvement in discipline concerns, scheduling issues, policy matters, faculty and staff relations and effective use of resources (NELP 4.4; PSEL 4.e)). Candidate is aware of his/

her administrative strengths and areas needed for growth.

Leadership Exit Interview and Final PowerPoint Presentation

NAME of CANDIDATE ADMISTRATOR

_____ DATE _____

UNIVERSITY ASSESSOR'S NAME

_____ SCORE _____

Exit Interview and Power Point Presentation Rubric

Criterion	Proficient (3)	Competent (2)	Developing (1)	Unacceptable (0)
Demonstrates Professional Values and Requirements NELP 8.1	Candidate Administrator completed 300 hours of administrative duties.	Candidate Administrator completed 290 to 299 hours of administrative duties	Candidate Administrator professionally completed no less than 275 hours of administrative duties	Candidate did not complete internship hours as required.
Professional Values and Standard Alignment NELP 1.2 PSEL 1.g	CA consistently modeled and advocated for core values of school's mission and vision. This was evidenced in very clear professional standard alignment with administrative involvement.	CA modeled and advocated for core values of school's mission and vision. This was evidenced in professional standard alignment with administrative involvement.	CA modeled and advocated for core values of school's mission and vision. Candidate was not able to show strong standard alignment with administrative involvement.	CA did not give evidence of modeling core values of school's mission and vision. CA lacked evidence of standard alignment.
Involvement in Support System NELP 1.3 PSEL 1.d	CA's presentation gave excellent evidence of active attendance in school improvement team, school board meetings, faculty and administrative meetings and duties (discipline decisions, academic support activities), and other duties as requested.	CA's presentation gave sufficient evidence of active attendance in school improvement team, school board meetings, faculty and administrative meetings and duties (discipline decisions, academic support activities), and other duties as requested.	CA's presentation gave some evidence of active attendance in school improvement team, school board meetings, faculty and administrative meetings and duties (discipline decisions, academic support activities), and other duties as requested.	CA 's presentation did not give sufficient evidence of involvement in required administrative duties.

Criterion	Proficient (3)	Competent (2)	Developing (1)	Unacceptable (0)
Responsive Practice NELP 3.3 PSEL 1.g	Change Project that addressed inequality of education or deficit surfaced in school improvement plan or alternative was carefully implemented and thoroughly sustained.	Change Project that addressed inequality of education or deficit surfaced in school improvement plan or alternative was implemented and sustained.	Change Project that addressed inequality of education or deficit surfaced in school improvement plan or alternative was implemented but not sufficiently sustained.	Change Project was not implemented.
Supports in Instructional Leadership NELP 4.4 PSEL 4.e	Change Project, and Academic Planning and Administrative Involvement effectively and efficiently incorporated resources (technology, faculty, staff, etc.).			
Effective Interaction and Communication NELP 5.1 PSEL 8.c	CA's gave clear evidence of very effective interaction with families and appropriate community entities. This was evident required artifact "Collaborating with Families", the Change Project and other school related activities.	CA's gave evidence of effective interaction with families and appropriate community entities. This was evident required artifact "Collaborating with Families", the Change Project and other school related activities.	CA's gave some evidence of very effective interaction with families and appropriate community entities. This was evident required artifact "Collaborating with Families", the Change Project and other school related activities.	CA did not give sufficient evidence of successful interactions with families and community entities.

Criterion	Proficient (3)	Competent (2)	Developing (1)	Unacceptable (0)
Team Leadership and Communication NELP 6.3 PSEL 7.e	Candidate clearly articulated and demonstrated team participation and clear communication in curricular involvement, such as, participation in grade/subject student data analysis, chair of department, coordinator of discipline, lead instructor for increased school improvement.	Candidate articulated and demonstrated team participation and communication in curricular involvement, such as, participation in grade/subject student data analysis, chair of department, coordinator of discipline, lead instructor for increased school improvement.	Candidate is developing in articulating and demonstrating team participation and communication in curricular involvement, such as, participation in grade/subject student data analysis, chair of department, coordinator of discipline, lead instructor for increased school improvement.	Candidate did not give evidence of successful participation and communication in measures involved in school improvement.
Improvement NELP 1.4 PSEL 1.e	Candidate gave excellent information that demonstrates consistent leadership engagement with faculty and staff using important and varied data to review, evaluate, and make necessary changes (e.g. change project and other academic implementations).	Candidate gave information that demonstrates leadership engagement with faculty and staff using varied data to review, evaluate, and make necessary changes (e. g. change project and other academic implementations).	Candidate gave some information of engagement with faculty and staff evaluating academics for purpose of improvement.	Candidate did not give sufficient information that gives evidence of engagement with faculty and staff to improve academics.

Criterion	Proficient (3)	Competent (2)	Developing (1)	Unacceptable (0)
Effectiveness of Presentation and Ability to Respond to Questions	Candidate's presentation was carefully, creatively, and professionally explained. Candidate responded to questions clearly and concisely using meaningful examples.	Candidate's presentation was clearly and professionally presented and he/she answered questions adequately	Candidate's presentation was effective, but lacked some clarity in the delivery and in responding to questions.	Candidate was inadequate in effectively presenting his/her experience.
Effective Use of Professional Terminology.	Candidate effectively and easily used educational terminology throughout the presentation. PowerPoint had no grammatical mistakes.	Candidate appropriately used educational terminology. PowerPoint had no grammatical mistakes.	Candidate used minimal educational terminology. PowerPoint had a few grammatical mistakes.	Candidate did not use appropriate educational terminology and/or had several written or grammatical errors.
Effective use of time	Candidate was exceptionally well organized and presented material within appropriate time frame (20 minutes).	Candidate was effective in the use of the required 20 minute time frame and was organized.	Candidate was organized but did not stay to the timeline.	Candidate's presentation was too brief or too long and not well organized
Appearance	Candidate was professionally dressed.	Candidate was appropriately dressed.	Candidate was somewhat appropriately dressed.	Candidate was not appropriately dressed

Criterion	Proficient (3)	Competent (2)	Developing (1)	Unacceptable (0)
Confidence and Organization	Candidate displayed a professional level of confidence and organization.	Candidate displayed confidence and organization.	Candidate displayed confidence but was not well organized or organized but not confident.	Candidate displayed inadequate confidence, was not well organized.
Professional Growth	Candidate clearly and insightfully identified administrative strengths and excellent areas needed for growth.	Candidate identified administrative strengths and areas needed for growth.	Candidate identified strengths and areas needed for growth.	

Appendices

Appendix A

Mentor Administrator Agreement Form

By signing this statement, I agree to supervise the candidate, _____, in his/her Practicum experience. The candidate and I have reviewed the requirements of this administrative internship, and have designed the experience according to our educational setting.

I am aware that candidate administrator is to have an active role in the School Improvement Team or its equivalent and that he/she is to be involved in on-going instructional planning with grade or subject level colleagues.

I will complete the appropriate evaluation forms at the mid-term and completion of the practicum experience.

_____

Mentor Administrator's Signature

_____

Title

_____

Principal's Signature

_____

Candidate Administrator's Signature

_____

Date

Appendix B

Approval Letter for Change Project

This letter is to verify that I am aware of and support the Change Project being proposed by _____ under my supervision. His/her project involving _____ _____ is practical and applicable to our school and its students. It is our goal to implement this program for our school community.

_____

Mentor Administrator's Signature

_____

Title

_____

Principal's Signature

_____

Candidate Administrator's Signature

_____

Date

Appendix C

Resources:

A. Download the National Educational Leadership Preparation Standards (NELP) from the following site: http://caepnet.org/

B. Download Professional Standards for Educational Leaders (PSEL) from the following site: http://www.npbea.org/wp/wp-content/uploads/2014/11/ProfessionalStandardsforEducationalLeaders2015forNPBEAFINAL-2.pdf

C. Download Technology Standards visit http://www.iste.org/standards

Maryland Department of Education visit: http://www.marylandpublic-schools.org/

Maryland Technology Standards for School Administrators visit: http://marylandpublicschools.org/MSDE/programs/technology/techstds/admin_standards.htm

Appendix D

Notre Dame of Maryland University
School of Education

RSVP-SEO Alignment

As individuals who care, listen to, understand, and respect one another, faculty and students together create a community of shared inquiry and embody the following commonly-shared values that we believe are inherent qualities of sound teaching and meaningful learning. We refer to this synergy as our **RSVP Conceptual Framework** from which are derived five specific School of Education Outcomes (SEOs) that are embedded in each of our teacher preparation programs. These outcomes are designed to prepare participants with the requisite skills needed to promote student achievement:

RSVP Conceptual Framework and Outcomes

Research

Research-based and experience-based teaching within a liberal arts tradition enables the educator to act with the integrity that comes from knowing what one is doing and why one is doing it.

Associated outcomes: (SEO-1) Demonstrate a general knowledge base in the liberal arts and in specific content appropriate for teaching and leading; and (SEO-2) Demonstrate effective application of principles derived from the ongoing relationship between research-informed theory and practice.

Self-Reflection

Reflection in action and critical self-knowledge enable the educator to articulate a point of view that is guided by informed reason rather than rhetoric, a personally appropriated value position, and attentive self-assessment.

Associated outcome: (SEO-3) Exemplify the qualities of a reflective practitioner and leader through analysis and assessment of teaching practices and behaviors, redesigning instruction to meet individual needs.

| **Vocation** | Teaching is a vocation or "calling" in which the meaning of professionalism gives equal weight to both competence and virtue. |

Associated outcome: (SEO-4) Act and make decisions guided by a philosophy of teaching and learning is rooted in a moral system that values the development and diversity of each individual.

Practice Teachers, who exhibit visionary leadership and commitment to life-long learning, apply exemplary educational practices, which encourage and enable others to act with imagination, risk-taking, intention, and invention.

Associated outcome: (SEO-5) Create a safe and interactive environment in which students are both empowered and free to take risks, to think analytically, critically, and creatively, to make informed choices and to act responsibly.

School of Education Objectives (SEOs)

From the Notre Dame of Maryland University's Conceptual Framework

1. Demonstrate a general knowledge based in the liberal arts and in specific content appropriate for teaching.
2. Demonstrate effective application of principles derived from the on-going relationship between research-informed theory and practice.
3. Exemplify the qualities of a reflective practitioner through analysis and assessment of teaching practices and behaviors, redesigning instruction to meet individual needs.
4. Act and make decisions guided by a philosophy of teaching and learning rooted in a moral system that values the development and diversity of each individual.
5. Create a safe and interactive environment in which students are both empowered and free to take risks, to think analytically, critically, and creatively, to make informed choices, and to act responsibility.

2 paragraphs

relationship to mission & vision of school

NLA building improvement plan

CPSIA information can be obtained
at www.ICGtesting.com
Printed in the USA
FSHW012324251019
63387FS